MW00957226

SAMSUNG
A14 5G USER MANUAL

A Complete User Guide for Beginners and
Seniors with Tips and Tricks to Master the
Galaxy A14 like a Pro

Gladys Newman

1

Table of Contents

Chapter One: Device Setup

The battery should be charged. A nano SIM card is used in your device.

It's possible that a SIM card will come preinstalled, or that you can use your old SIM card.

For further information, contact the carrier.

Note that local and federal guidelines and limits may apply to the usage of mobile devices aboard a ship.

Always check with the relevant authorities and follow the crew's instructions on how and when to use your gadget.

Battery Charging

A rechargeable battery powers your smartphone.

Note that you should use only Samsung-approved charging batteries and devices (where applicable) (where applicable).

These gadgets are specifically built for your phone to help you get the most out of your battery life. Using alternative batteries and charging devices can void its warranty and cause harm. The charger and its device can become hot during charging and cease charging.

Install SIM/microSD card
Place the SIM card and optional microSD card (sold separately) into the tray with the gold contacts facing down.

Charge your device
Before turning on your device, charge it fully.

This normally has no effect on the device's performance or lifespan, and it is within its regular operating range. Be patient enough for the heat on the device to dissipate before disconnecting the charger.

Get started with your device

Switch on your smartphone

To turn on your smartphone, press the Side key. If the device is not in good working order, don't use it.

After the device is repaired, you can use it. To turn on the gadget, hold down the Side key.

• Hold down the Side key then Power off to turn off the device. When prompted, confirm.

• Hold down the Side key then press Restart to restart your device. When prompted, confirm.

Make use of the Setup Wizard

The Setup Wizard walks you through the device's basics settings when you first switch it on.

Connect to Wi-Fi, select a language, configure accounts, select location services, know more about the features of device, and more by following the instructions.

Data Transfer from an old phone

Transfer pictures, contacts, music, messages, videos, calendars, notes, and other files from an old device with Smart Switch™. Your data can be transferred via Smart Switch through Wi-Fi, USB cable, or a computer.

1. Select Accounts and Backup then Smart Switch from the Settings menu.

2. Choose the content that you want to transfer by following the prompts.

Locking and unlocking your device

For your device's security, use the screen lock's features. Upon screen time out, the device will automatically lock by default.

Side key
Press to lock.
Press to turn on the
screen, and then
swipe the screen to
unlock it.

Settings for the Side Key

The Side Key's shortcuts can be changed.

Double Press

When you press the Side key twice, you can choose which functionality is launched.

1. Select Advanced features then Side key from the Settings menu.

2. Double-tap to activate this feature, then tap one of the following options:

• Launch app

• Quick camera launch

Accounts

Configure and manage your accounts. Note that calendars, contacts, email, and other functions may be supported by accounts.

Register for a Google Account

Log into your Google Account to have access to your Google Cloud Storage, installed apps, and take advantage of all of your Android™ device's features.

1. Select Accounts and backup then Accounts from the Settings menu.

2. Select Google from the Add Account menu.

Note that Factory Reset Protection (FRP) is enabled if you log into a Google Account.

When you reset your phone to factory settings, FRP asks for your Google Account credentials.

Setup a Samsung account

Log in to your Samsung account to gain access to unique Samsung content and to enjoy Samsung apps fully.

1. Go to Settings then Accounts and backup then Accounts.

2. Select Add account then Samsung account.

Add a Microsoft Outlook account

To read and manage your email messages, log in to your Outlook® account.

1. Go to Settings then Accounts and backup then Accounts.

2. Select Add Account then Outlook.

Configure voicemail

The first time you use it, you can configure your voicemail service.

Voicemail can be accessed via the Phone app. Options differ depending on the carrier.

1. From the Phone, press and hold the 1 key, or press Voicemail.

2. Follow the on-screen instructions to record a greeting, setup a password, or record your name. A light touch from a capacitive stylus or your finger pad or works best on a touch screen.

Excessive force or the use of a metallic object may cause damage to the screen's surface, which will void the warranty.

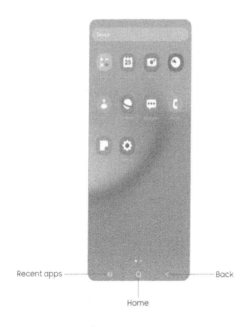

Recent apps ----- Back

Home

Buttons for navigation

To navigate quickly, use the buttons at the screen's bottom.

1. Go to Settings then Display then Navigation bar then Buttons.

2. Select an option under Button order to determine where the Recent and Back apps icons appear on the screen.

Gestures for navigation

Place the buttons for navigation at the screen's bottom to get a clear view of the screen.

Swipe instead to navigate the display.

1. To enable this feature, go to Settings then Display then Navigation bar then Swipe gestures.

2. To customize, select one of the following options:

• Additional options: Select a gesture type and sensitivity level.

• Gesture hints: Show the lines at the screen's bottom indicating the location of each screen gesture.

• Show keyboard hide button: When the phone is in portrait mode, display an icon in the screen's bottom right corner to conceal the keyboard.

The Home screen is the starting point for navigating your device.

You can place your favorite apps and widgets here, in addition to setting up additional Home screens, removing screens, changing the order of screens, and choosing a main Home screen.

Personalize your home screen

This Home screen is where you begin navigating the device. You can choose a primary Home screen, add new Home screens, delete screens, change the order of the screens, and add your favorite widgets and apps here.

Mobile application icons

Use the app icon to launch an app from the Home screen.

- Tap Add to Home after holding down an app icon in the Apps section.
- Hold down an app icon on a Home screen and select Remove from Home to remove it.
- It should be noted that removing an icon from the Home screen does not delete the associated app; rather, it merely removes the icon from view.

Wallpaper

To change the appearance of the Lock Screen and Home, select a favorite image, movie, or preloaded wallpaper.

Hold the screen down while selecting Wallpaper from the Home screen in order to view the available wallpapers.

• My wall décor: Choose from a variety of featured and downloaded wallpapers.

• Gallery: Choose photos and videos that have been saved in the app's Gallery section.

• Wallpaper services: Turn on supplemental options like Dynamic Lock Screen and the help page.

• Use Dark Mode on Wallpaper: Turn on Dark Mode for your background image.

• See additional wallpapers: You can view and download additional Galaxy Themes wallpapers here.

1. Tap a video or image to select it.

• If you're using a single image, choose which screen you want the wallpaper to appear on.

• The Lock screen can only be utilized with videos and multiple photos.

• Tap on any things in the Gallery to choose movies or pictures, then click Done.

2. Decide whether to set the screen to be on the lock, the home, or both.

• If you want to apply any changes you make to the wallpaper on both the Lock and Home screens while using a photo from the Gallery, turn on Sync my edits.

Themes

Pick a theme for your app icons, wallpaper, and Lock and Home screens.

1. Keep the screen from the Home screen pressed down.
2. Select a theme to view and download by tapping Themes.
3. To view the themes you've downloaded, go to the Navigation drawer, followed by My things and Themes.
4. After selecting a theme, click Apply to put it into use.

Icons

Use different icon sets to change the standard icons.
1. From any Home screen, hold down the screen.
2. Select an icon set to examine and download by going to Themes, then Icons.
3. To view the icons you've downloaded, go to the Navigation drawer, followed by My Stuff and Icons.
4. To apply the icon set you've selected, click an icon and then Apply.

Widget

Your home screens can be customized with widgets to give you quick access to apps and information.

1. Take a screenshot of the Home screen.
2. Click on Widgets, then click on a widget set to add it.
3. Drag the chosen widget to a Home screen by swiping to it.

Customization of a widget

You can alter a widget's appearance and functionality after you've created it.

When you press an option while holding down a widget on the Home screen:

• Deleting a widget from the home screen.

• Change the widget's settings to alter its appearance or functionality.

• App information: Look over the usage, widget permission, and other information.

Default settings for the home page
You may customize how your Apps and Home screens look.
1. Starting on the Home screen, hold down the screen.
2. Select Settings > Home Screen to alter the look of your home screen.
• Home screen layout: You can set up your smartphone to have separate Apps and Home displays or to have just one Home screen that contains all of your apps.
• Home screen grid: Choose a layout to modify the arrangement of icons on a Home screen.
• Grid on the Apps screen: Choose a layout to modify how icons show on the Apps screen.
• Apps button: Add a button to the Home screen for easy access to the Apps screen.
Activate the display of app icon badges for those that have active notifications. Additionally, you can choose a badge style.

• Home Lock Screen Layout: Prevent the moving or deletion of Home screen elements.

• Add apps to the Home screen: Automatically add recently downloaded apps to a Home screen.

• Swipe down for a notification panel: Enabling this option enables you to slide down on the Home screen to access the Notification panel.

• Rotate to landscape mode: When your smartphone switches from portrait to landscape orientation, a Home screen will automatically rotate.

• Secretive apps: You can choose which apps to remove from the App and Home displays.

Return to this screen to reveal the hidden apps.

The hidden apps are still present and will come up in Finder search results.

Panel of notifications

To get quick access to settings, notifications, and more, just open the Notification panel.

Quick settings

Device settings

Notification cards

View the Notifications panel

Any screen can access the Notification panel.

1. To display the Notifications panel, swipe down from the top of the screen. To open an item, tap it.

• Drag a single notice to the right or left to get rid of it.

• To delete all of the notifications, select clear.

• To customize notifications, click Notification settings.

2. Drag the Notifications panel up from the bottom of the screen or touch Back to close it.

Gestures captured by a finger sensor

The Notification panel may be opened or closed by swiping down or up on the fingerprint sensor.

1. Choose Advanced features, and then, motions and gestures. From the Settings menu, use finger sensor gestures.

2. Tap to make the feature active.

Fast Settings

The Notification panel provides rapid access to device activities through Quick settings.

With two fingers, swipe down from the top of the screen to uncover Quick settings.

• Tap Finder search to perform a device search.

• To access the Emergency mode, Power off, and Restart options, tap Power off.

To quickly access the device's settings menu, tap Open settings.

• Click More choices to change the button's design or the Quick settings' hierarchy.

• By tapping the Quick setting icon, you can turn it on or off.

• Press and hold any quick setting symbol to access a setting.

• To alter the screen's brightness, use the Brightness slider.

Samsung Free

Free access to articles from various sources, live TV, news, interactive games, and live TV shows.

- From any Home screen, swipe right.
- To customize Samsung Free, select More options and then Settings.

Parental controls and online safety

By getting a daily summary of your app usage patterns, the number of alerts you receive, and how often you check your device, you can monitor and control your online behaviors.

Additionally, you may set up your device to help you get ready for bed.

From the Settings menu, select Parental Control and Digital Wellbeing to get the following features:

• Visit the Dashboard to see the information below: Screen time: Check how long an app is opened and used each day.

View the daily total of notifications you receive from a given app. See when an app has been unlocked throughout the day.

Those are your goals

• Screen time: Set a daily average for your screen time and monitor it.

• Unlocks: Determine how often you want to unlock your device each day and view your daily average.

• App timers: Establish a cap on the amount of time you spend using each app.

Disconnection Methods

• Focus mode: To prevent device distractions, set time limitations for app usage.

• Wind down: Limit alerts and enable the screen to go grayscale before night. Keep an eye on your kids.

• Parental controls: Keep an eye on your kids' online activities by using the Google Family Link app.

You may choose apps, use content filters, keep track of screen time, and set screen time restrictions.

Biometrics

Use biometrics to securely log into your accounts and unlock your smartphone.

Face Identification

The screen may be unlocked by turning on face recognition.

You must first set a PIN, pattern, or password in order to unlock the device using your face.

• Compared to a PIN, a password, or a pattern, face recognition is less secure.

Your device might be unlocked by anything or someone who resembles your image.

• Some situations, such as wearing hats, glasses, beards, or even a lot of makeup, may make it difficult to recognize faces.

• Ensure that the camera lens is clean and that you are in a well-lit area when performing the face registration.

1. Select Settings, followed by Biometrics and security, and finally Face recognition.

2. Comply with the face registration instructions displayed on the screen.

Control over face recognition

The operation of facial recognition is modifiable.

• From the Settings menu, select Biometrics and security, then Face recognition.

• Eliminate Face Data: Delete the current faces.

• Alter your appearance: To make it easier to identify faces, alter your appearance.

• Face unlocking allows you to turn on or off face recognition security.

• Remain in the Lock screen: If you're using facial recognition to unlock your device, don't swipe the screen until you've finished.

• Quicker recognition: Turn on this setting to enable face recognition more quickly.

To increase protection and make it more challenging to open with a video or image of your likeness, turn it off.

• Eyes must be open: In order for facial recognition to work, your eyes must be wide open.

• Increase screen brightness momentarily to help you recognize your face in dimly lit areas.

• In relation to biometric unlocking: Learn more about securing your smartphone with biometrics.

Reader for fingerprints

You can use fingerprint recognition in some applications in place of inputting passwords.

Your fingerprint can be used to verify your identity when logging into your Samsung account.

You must first create a PIN, pattern, or password in order to unlock a device with your fingerprint.

1. Select Settings, Biometrics and Security, and Fingerprints from the menu.

2. Comply with the fingerprint registration instructions displayed on the screen.

Administration of fingerprints

It is possible to add, remove, and rename fingerprints. To access the following menus, tap Settings, then Biometrics and Security, then Fingerprints.

• A list of registered fingerprints is shown at the top. By tapping a fingerprint, you can change its name or delete it.

• Add a fresh fingerprint: To register a fresh fingerprint, simply adhere to the guidelines.

• Verify the additional fingerprints: To find out if the fingerprints have already been registered, scan them.

Settings for fingerprint verification

Use fingerprint recognition in activities and apps that support it to verify your identity.

From the Settings menu, select Biometrics and Security, then Fingerprints.

• Fingerprint unlock: Use your fingerprint to identify the smartphone when you want to unlock it.

• Fingerprints are constantly active

Your device will wake up and then unlock by simply touching the Side key.

• Web sign-in: Use your fingerprints to log into various websites.

• Samsung account: Use your fingerprints to verify your identity rather than your Samsung account password.

• For biometric unlocking, familiarize yourself with the conditions for using a

PIN, pattern, or password as a backup for each biometric security feature.

Settings for biometrics

Choose the biometric security features you want.

• From the Settings menu, choose Biometrics and security, then Biometrics options.

• Screen transition effect: Show a transition when using biometrics to unlock a smartphone.

Many windows

In order to multitask, use many programs simultaneously.

Applications that are supported by Multi windowTM can be displayed side by side on a split screen.

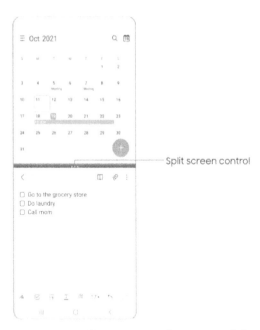

Split screen control

You can adjust window widths and switch between apps.

1. From any screen, choose Recent Apps.

2. After selecting Open in split screen mode, tap an app icon.

3. Tap an app from the opposite window to bring it into the split screen view.

• Drag the center of the window's border to alter the size.

Window configuration

In split screen mode, the Window controls affect how app windows look.

1. Drag the window border's center to resize the windows.

2. Press the middle of the window's border to access the following options.

• Switch the windows: Alternate the two windows.

Text Entry You can type text using a keyboard or your voice.

Toolbar

Keyboard functionality is easily accessible from the toolbar. Depending on the carrier, options could be different.

The following options will appear when you tap Expand toolbar on the Samsung keyboard:

• Emojis: Include one.

• Stickers: Offer graphic stickers.

GIFs: Consist of animated GIFs.

• Voice input: To type, use Google VoiceTM.

Access the keyboard's settings by going to the settings menu.

• Search: Look for specific words or phrases in your speeches.

• Translate: Type phrases and words into another language using the keyboard.

• Text editing: You may find text to copy, cut, and paste by using an editing panel.

Select a keyboard layout under "Modes."

• Keyboard dimensions: Alter the keyboard's height and width.

The Samsung keyboard set up

Set up the Samsung keyboard according to your preferences. To access the following options, tap Settings on the Samsung keyboard:

• Keyboard styles and languages: Set the keyboard type and the keyboard languages you want to use. Language switching is accomplished by right- or left-swiping the Space bar.

• Smart typing: Use predictive text and auto-correction tools to prevent common typing errors.
Typing is done by swiping between letters.
• Format and design: Modify the keyboard's appearance and functionality.
• Change the motions and feedback via swiping, feedback, and touching.
• Features of third-party keyboards: Enable the capability of the external keyboard.
• Reset the keyboard to its default settings and remove any personalized information.
With regards to the Samsung keyboard: View the legal information and version of the Samsung keyboard.
• Speak with us: For support, get in touch with Samsung Members.
Type using Google Voice
Rather than typing, speak the text.

Open Settings — Return to keyboard

Tap to speak

Google

1. Choosing voice input on the Samsung keyboard.

2. Say your text after tapping the screen.

Change Google Voice's typing settings

1. Choosing voice input on the Samsung keyboard is step one.

2. Visit Settings to see your choices. Choose a keyboard language under "Languages."

• Google Voice typing languages can be downloaded for offline use to enable offline speech recognition.

• Delete words that could be offensive: To obfuscate terms that may offend, use asterisks.

In crisis mode

Use Emergency mode to gain access to helpful emergency resources and preserve the battery life of your device in an emergency.

To save battery life, go to the Emergency Mode:

• Select only the necessary apps from the available list.

• When the display is off, mobile data and connectivity features are disabled.

Turn on emergency mode

1. Press Power while on the Notifications panel to activate Emergency mode.

2. Hit the Emergency Mode button.

• Read the terms and conditions for the first time and agree to them.

3. Select the Emergency mode features button.

The Home Screen will include the following features and applications when in Emergency mode:

• Flashlight: Use the flash as a source of light.

• Siren to sound in case of emergency.

• Share my location: Let the people who can help you in an emergency know where you are.

• Phone: Access the dialing screen. Enter the browser for the internet.

• Add: Choose more applications to display on the Emergency mode screen.

• Battery charge: Display the battery's estimated percentage of charge.

• Estimated battery life: Based on the battery's usage and charge at the time, display how long the battery is expected to last.

• In an emergency, contact 911 or another appropriate number. This call can be placed without a network.

Other choices

• Disable Emergency mode: Disable Emergency mode and return to normal mode.

• Removing apps: Choose the ones you don't want to see on the screen.

• Emergency contacts: Maintain your ICE (In Case of Emergency) and medical profile group connections.

• Settings: Configure your settings.

In Emergency mode, just a few settings are accessible.

Turn off emergency mode

Your device will return to ordinary mode if emergency mode is turned off.

Chapter Two: Apps

The Apps list shows all installed and downloaded apps. Both the Google Play Store and the Galaxy Store provide downloadable apps.

- Swipe the screen up from the Home screen to view the Apps list.

Disable or remove applications

You can uninstall any installed apps from your smartphone. Some preloaded (or pre-installed) apps on your smartphone can simply be disabled.

Disabled apps are turned off and eliminated from the list of apps.

- In Apps, while holding down an app, select Uninstall/Disable.

Obtain apps

If you don't know where to seek for a setting or program, use the Search function.

1. Click Search in the Apps menu, then enter a word. As you type, the screen will show results for settings and apps that match.

2. Tap a result to launch an application.

You can modify the search settings by going to the Finder settings and selecting more choices.

App sorting

App shortcuts can be arranged however you choose, whether alphabetically or in any other arrangement.

- To get the following choices, select Apps, then click More Options, followed by Sort:
- Custom Order: Arrange apps manually.
- Alphabetical Order: Sort apps according to their names.

When manually arranging apps (Custom order), empty icon spaces can be removed by selecting More options, then Clean up pages.

How to Make and Use New Folders

You can make folders to organize App shortcuts on the Apps list.

1. From the Apps menu, choose an app shortcut and drag it onto another app shortcut until it becomes highlighted.

2. Keep the app shortcut and create a folder.

- Name the folder by providing a name.
- Palette: Alter the folder's color.
- Add Apps: Boost the quantity of applications in a folder. Tap the apps you want to select, then tap Done.

3. Tap Back to leave the folder.

Copy a folder to a Home screen

By copying a folder, you can add it to a Home screen.

- A Home screen can receive a copy of a folder. In Apps, while holding down a folder, select Add to Home.

Folder removal

After a folder has been deleted, an app shortcut returns to the list of apps.

1. When prompted, choose Delete Folder, and then confirm the deletion.

An enhancer for gaming

Receive optimum game performance based on your usage.

Turn on features like Bixby and Dolby Atmos, block incoming calls and notifications, and so forth.

When playing a game, swipe up from the bottom of the screen to see the navigation bar.

The following options can be found on the left and right sides:

- Screen touch lock: Lock the screen to avoid unintentional tapping. This is the usual configuration.

- Game Booster: You may adjust a number of settings, including performance tracking and blocking screen touches, the menu bar, and snapshots.

The app's settings

Organize the downloaded and installed apps on your device. Apps come in a variety of forms.

1. From the Settings menu, choose Apps.

2. Select the More option to bring up the following options:

- Order by: Sort apps according to their name, size, most recent usage, or most recent update.
- Default apps: Choose or change the default apps for specific tasks, such email or web browsing.
- Permissions manager: Control which apps on your smartphone have access to certain features.
- Show/Hide system apps: You have the option of displaying or hiding background programs.
- Special access: Select which applications have access to certain functionalities on your device.

- Reset preferences for the app: Reset any recently modified settings. There is no deletion of data from previously installed apps.

3. Tap an app to view and/or edit its information.

The following choices could be seen:

- Mobile data: Check the amount of data your phone is using.
- Battery: Check the amount of power utilized since the last full charge.
- Storage: Manage how much room the software occupies.
- Memory: Check your current memory use.
- Notifications: To configure notifications, use the app.
- Permissions: Check the app's access rights to the data on your smartphone.
- Set as default: Establish the app as the standard in a certain app category.
- There are various possibilities in apps.

Informational options for apps

- Open: Launch the program. Some apps don't have access to this capability.
- Disable/Uninstall: The software can be removed or disabled. Some pre-installed apps can only be disabled; they cannot be deleted.
- Force stop: Stop a malfunctioning app. The apps on the following list are either downloaded or preloaded onto your device during setup.

They are available for download through the Galaxy shop or Playstore.

Samsung Store

Find and install exclusive premium apps for Samsung Galaxy phones. You'll need a Samsung account to download from the Galaxy Store.

From the Apps menu, select Galaxy Store.

Launched a game

Put all of your games in one easy-to-find place. From the Apps menu, select the Samsung folder and then Game Launcher.

Galaxy Free

Get free access to a variety of sources' articles, news, live TV, and games.

Samsung's Global Objective

You can learn more about the Global Goals initiative and donate to causes that support them by watching the advertisements on this app.

Galaxy Members

Utilize your Galaxy device to the fullest. Only Samsung members get access to DIY support resources, unique opportunities, and knowledge.

Your smartphone could already have Samsung Members pre-installed, or you can download it from the Galaxy Store or Google Play.

Calculator

The Calculator app has capabilities for both scientific and common math, as well as a unit converter.

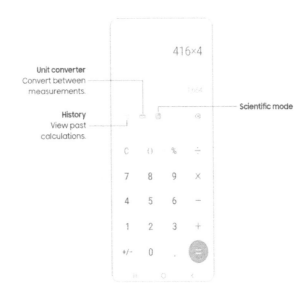

Calendar

You can sync your calendars from all of your internet accounts with the Calendar app. Calendar can be found under the Apps menu.

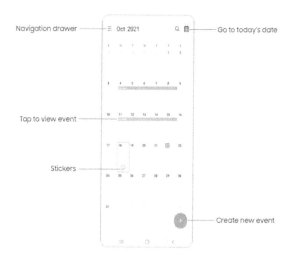

Navigation drawer ──── ≡ Oct 2021   Q 📅 ──── Go to today's date

Tap to view event ────

Stickers ────

──── Create new event

Calendar Add

You need to first add your accounts in order to utilize the Calendar app.

1. From the Calendar, open the Navigation drawer.

2. Select an account type and add a new account by going to Calendar settings.

3. After entering your account details, follow the on-screen directions. Contact, email, and other features may be available on accounts.

Calendar alert types

The alarms in the Calendar app come in a number of designs.

1. From the Calendar app, select Navigation drawer, Calendar settings, and Alert style.

There are a number of options available:

- Light: A brief sound will then alert you.
- Medium: First, hear a brief sound followed by a full-screen alert.
- Strong: You'll first hear a ringing sound that won't stop unless you reject a full-screen alert.

2. Depending on the type of alarm you chose, you can choose from the sounds below:

- Ring Once: Choose from the Medium or Light alarm types' alert tones.
- Continue ringing: Choose the alert sound for the Strong alert style.

Create an Event

By utilizing your calendar, create events.

1. Click Add event on the Calendar page to add an event.

2. Complete the event's information and click Save.

Remove a certain occurrence

Removing upcoming activities from the calendar.

1. Tap an event in the Calendar, then tap it once more to make changes.

2. Tap Delete and confirm Clock when requested. You may track time and set alarms with the app.

Clock

To use a feature, select Apps, then Clock, and finally any tab.

Alarm in 2 hours
57 minutes
Fri, Oct 22, 5:30 PM

Add alarm

Turn alarm on or off

6:00 AM

12:00 PM

5:30 PM

Alarm   World clock   Stopwatch   Timer

Alarm

Using the Alarm tab, set one-time or recurring alarms and then select the notification method.

1. Choose Add alarm from the Clock option.

2. Select one of the following options to set an alarm:

- Set the alarm for a particular time.
- Choose the days you want your alarm to go off.
- Alarm name: Describe the alarm.

- Alarm sound: Choose a sound for the alarm to play, then use the slider to change the level.
- Vibration: Decide if the alarm should vibrate.
- Snooze: Allow for sleeping. Set the interval and repetition settings for the alarm while you're asleep.

3. Press Save to save an alarm.

Unplug the alarm

An alarm that you've put up can be removed.

1. Depress an alarm from the clock.

2. Press Delete.

Setting up alerts

Even if the Sound mode is set to Vibrate or Mute, you can configure the phone to vibrate for timers and alarms.

1. Click More options, then Settings, on the clock.

2. To turn on this feature, press the Vibrate for Timer and Alarm button.

World time

You can check the time in many cities across the world using the World Clock.

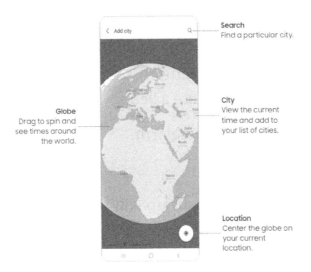

Search
Find a particular city.

Globe
Drag to spin and see times around the world.

City
View the current time and add to your list of cities.

Location
Center the globe on your current location.

Stopwatch

The stopwatch allows you to time events to the hundredth of a second.

1. From the Clock menu, choose Stopwatch.

2. To start the timer, press Start. To track lap times, press Lap.

3. To stop the timer, press Stop.

• To restart timing after stopping the clock, tap Resume.

• To reset it to zero, press Reset.

Timer

Set a timer for 99 days, 59 minutes, and 59 seconds.

1. From the Clock menu, choose Timer.

2. On the keypad, touch Seconds, Minutes, and Hours to set the timer.

3. Tap Start to start the timer.

• To pause the Timer momentarily, press Pause. To proceed, click Resume.

4. To halt and restart the timer, press Cancel.

Built-in timer

You can name and store preset timings.

1. From the Clock menu, choose Timer, followed by Add preset timer.

2. Choose a name for the timer and the start time.

3. Press Add to save.

- Select More choices
- Edit preset timers to make changes to a saved preset timing

A timer's options

Custom parameters are available for the timer.

1. From the Clock menu, choose Timer.

2. Choose More choices followed by Settings.

• Sound: Choose from one of the preset sounds or record your own.

• Vibration: Select this option to disable the timer's vibration.

Default settings

The settings for all Clock tools can be examined and modified.

Select Settings from the Clock menu's More choices.

• Vibrate for timers and alarms: The timers and alarms will always vibrate when the Sound mode is set to Vibrate or Mute.

• Material personalization service: Sign into your Samsung account to edit content in apps that support it.

• Timekeeping: Verify the software version and check for updates.

Contacts

Manage and keep track of your contacts. The device's personal accounts that have been added can be synced. Accounts may grant access to calendars, email, and other features.

Add profile picture

Add, delete, and expand fields

Contact someone

Select Create contact from the Apps menu, then select Contacts.

Change a contact

You may edit or delete information by pressing any field. While modifying a contact, you can also add additional fields to the contact's information list.

1. Choose a contact from the list of contacts.

2. Choose Edit.

3. Tap any field to add, edit, or remove information.

4. Choose Save.

Favorites

Popular contacts are conveniently accessible from other apps.

1. Choose a contact from the list of contacts.

2. To add the contact to your favorites list, choose Add to Favorites.

To remove a contact from the Favorites list, tap Remove from Favorites.

Contact Sharing

Exchange contacts with others by using a variety of sharing tools and services.

1. Choose a contact from the list of contacts.

2. Click on Share.

3. Choose Text or File.

4. Choose a sharing method and follow the steps displayed on the screen.

Press the QR code to instantly share a contact's details with loved ones after viewing them.

The QR code automatically updates as you change the contact details.

Share Directly

You may instantly share anything with your contacts from any app. Your frequently used contacts will appear in the Share tab once you've enabled it.

Navigate to Settings, select Advance features, and then group shares directly.

Delete or add group contacts

Your contacts can be arranged by forming groups.

Create a group

Create contact lists.

1. Click Contacts, and then go to the Contacts menu, then select Groups.

2. Select Create group, then select Fields to enter the group's details:

• Group name: Specify a name for the new team.

•Group ringtone: Play a sound for the group.

• To add a member, choose the contacts you want to be a part of the new group, and then click Done.

3. Select the "Save" option.

Add or delete contact from group

1. Change the group's contacts by adding or removing them as needed.
2. Press Groups from Contacts, then Open drawer, and finally a group.

• Touch and hold a contact to select it, then press Remove to erase it.

• To add a contact, select Edit > Add Member > Tap the names of the individuals you want to include.

3. When finished, select Done and then Save.

Contact a Group

Send a text message to several persons.

1. Select a group by going to Contacts, Open Drawer, then Groups.
2. Choose Send message, then choose More options.

Send an email to the group

1. Select a group by going to Contacts, pressing Open Drawer, Groups, and selecting that group.

2. Select More choices and then Email.

3. Tap contacts to pick them, or tap the All checkbox at the top of the screen to select all of them. Only group members with recorded email addresses will be displayed.

4. After choosing an email address, follow the on-screen directions.

Take a group away

Remove a group you've created.

1. Select a group by going to Contacts, Open Drawer, and Groups.

2. Click More choices, then click Delete.

- If you only want to delete a group, choose Group only.
- Press Group and Members to remove both the group and its members.

Control contacts

A contact record can contain several linked contacts, and contacts can be exported or imported.

Bring in contact details

Contacts can be imported onto your smartphone using card files.

1. Select Manage contacts from the Contacts menu, then select Open drawer.

2. Click Contacts Export or Import.

3. Select Import, then adhere to the prompts on the screen.

Exporting contact details

The contacts on your device can be exported as card files.

1. Select Manage contacts from the Contacts menu, then select Open drawer.

2. Click Contacts Export or Import.

3. Click Export and adhere to the directions displayed on the screen.

Contact sync

You can merge contact details from various sources into a single contact by integrating entries into it.

1. Tap the contact to choose it from the Contacts list.

2. Choose Sync.

Configure the Default Storage

Your new contacts can be instantly saved to your SIM, an account, or a device.

1. Select Manage Contact under Contacts, then select Open Drawer.

2. Click Default Storage.

3. Select an option to utilize a different account or the default one.

Removing contacts

A contact or a collection of contacts can be deleted.

1. Select a contact from the list of contacts by touching and holding it. You may also tap other contacts to select them for deletion.

2. Select Delete and then confirm when prompted.

Internet

Samsung Internet is a quick, easy, and reliable mobile web browser. A more secure web browsing experience is offered through Biometric Web Login, Secret Mode, and Contents Blocker. Internet may be found under the Apps menu.

Web browser tabs

Use tabs to see many web pages at once.

- From the Internet menu, select Tabs, then New Tab. To close a tab, select Tabs, then Close Tab.

Recommend creating

Create bookmarks for your favorite pages to easily access them.

- Open the internet and select "bookmark" to save the current page.

Pull up a bookmark

Open a website from the Bookmarks page.

1. From the Internet menu, choose Bookmarks.

2. After choosing a bookmark entry, press it.

Save the website

The Internet app offers a variety of choices for saving webpages.

- To access any of the following options, select Tools, then Add page from the Internet app.
- Bookmarks: Add a website to your list of favorites.
- For quick access, check out your list of bookmarked or regularly visited websites.

- Home screen: Create a shortcut to a website on the Home screen.
- Saved pages: Save the webpage's content to the device so that it can be accessed while the device is offline.

Browse History

Get a list of the websites you've recently visited:

- From the Internet app, choose Tools, and then click History.

To remove your internet history, select More choices followed by Remove history.

Linked pages

Websites can be shared with contacts.

- Follow the on-screen directions after selecting Share from the Tools menu on the Internet.

Hidden Mode

Pages viewed in Secret mode don't leave any traces on your computer, such as cookies or browser history.

Compared to standard tab windows, secret tabs are deeper in color. The downloaded files will stay on your device even after you close a secret tab.

1. Select Tabs then Secret mode when using the Internet.

2. Press Start to begin browsing in Secret mode.

Configuring Secret Mode

Using the secret mode requires a biometric lock or password.

1. Select Internet, followed by Tabs.

2. To access the following menu, select More options, then Secret mode settings.

• Password protection: Create a password to access secret mode.

• Face: Use face recognition to keep the secret mode private.

• Fingerprints: Use a fingerprint scanner to keep the secret mode private.

• Clear the secret mode and return to the default settings. In order to turn off Secret mode, do the following:

- Hold Tabs then Turn off the Internet's Secret mode.
- Change the Internet settings for the Internet application.
- From the Internet menu, choose Tools, followed by Settings.

Messages

You may share images, send emojis, or just say hi to your contacts with the Messages app.

Message Lookup

Use the search function to quickly find a message.

1. From the Messages menu, choose Search.

2. In the search area, enter some terms and then press the Search key on your keyboard.

Get rid of discussions

You can remove interactions from the conversion history.

1. From the Messages menu, select More choices, then Delete.

2. Tap on each discussion that you want to remove.

3. Select Delete, then confirm when requested.

Emergency Information

If there are any threats or other problems that are urgent, you will be sent emergency alerts. It costs nothing to get an emergency alert message.

1. Choose Connections, and then from the Settings menu, further connection settings.

2. To customize emergency alert alerts, first choose Wireless Emergency Alerts, then Settings.

Send out SOS alerts

Send a message with your location to your approved contacts in case of an emergency.

1. Choose Advanced features, and then from the Settings menu, send SOS messages.

• To choose the number of times to press the Side key to send an SOS message, press 3 or 4.

• Select a contact by pressing Auto call someone to have them phoned once you send an SOS message.

• Click Attach photos to include a picture taken with both the front and back cameras.

• To include a five-second sound recording in the SOS message, click Attach audio recording.

• Click Messages Send. By creating new contacts or selecting from your Contacts, you can include recipients.

2. To send an SOS message, quickly hit the Side key three or four times.

Setting up messages

Set your text message and multimedia options.

• Select Settings from the Messages menu, then select More choices.

Emergency warnings

You will receive emergency warnings when there are risks or other problems. It costs nothing to receive an emergency alert message.

1. From the Messages menu, choose More options, followed by Settings.

2. To modify emergency alert alerts, choose Emergency alert settings.

My Files

You may view and manage files on your device, including pictures, music, videos, and sound snippets. You can see and manage data stored on your SD card and cloud accounts, if supported.

Group files

The files on the device are separated into the following groups:

• Recent files: View recently accessed files.

• Sort your files into categories using categories.

• Storage: You may access files on your SD card, cloud account, and smartphone. Your cloud account's type is determined by the services you utilize.

• Look through your storage to see what's using up space.

Options for My Files

Go to My Files to clear, change, and search the file history, among other things. From My Files, you can access the following options:

• Search: Find a file or folder.

• More options

An online service

Link to a cloud carrier service if one is available.

Look through your storage:

Determine what is taking up space.

Trash: Select whether to restore deleted files or permanently trash them. You can access the app's settings here.

Make contact with us:

Relate to other Samsung Members.

Phone

More than just placing calls is possible with the Phone app. Look into the specialized calling choices. Call your carrier for further details.

Calls

You can make and take calls from the Recents tab, Home screen, Contacts, and other places in the Phone app.

Call a number

You may place and receive phone calls from a Home screen. Hit Call from the Phone menu after entering a phone number on the keypad.

• Tap Keypad if you can't see the keypad.

Activate

Tap to dial

Swipe a contact or number to the right to dial them.

1. Select Settings, followed by Advanced features then gestures and movements

2. Swipe to dial a number or send a text message. Turn this function on or off.

Utilizing Recents to dial

All missed, incoming, and departing calls are recorded in the call log.

1. To view a list of recent calls, select Recents from the Phone menu in step one.
2. After choosing Call, choose a contact. From your Contacts list, dial a number.

Call a contact using Contacts. Swipe across a contact in Contacts to call them by doing so.

Call a friend

When you call, the phone will ring, and the caller's name or phone number will be shown.

The incoming call is displayed in a pop-up window if you're using an app. Move Answer to the right on the call screen to respond. Press Answer on the call pop-up screen to accept the call.

Decline a call

You can choose to reject an incoming call.

- If you're using an app, a pop-up screen will show you when a call comes in. To decline the call and send it to voicemail, drag Decline to the left on the call screen.

To decline the call and send it to voicemail, click Decline on the pop-up window. Message me if you wish to reject this. You can turn down a call by texting a message.

Select a message by dragging the Send message option up from the incoming call screen. On the call pop-up screen, select a message by pressing the Send message button.

The act of ending a call

Tap End call when you're ready to end the call.

Decisions made during a call

You can adjust the volume, perform other tasks, and switch between a speaker and a headset while on a call.

- Pressing the Volume keys will change the volume up or down.

Use a speaker or a headset instead

To hear a call, use the speaker or a Bluetooth headset.

- Press Bluetooth to hear the caller through a Bluetooth headset, or Speaker to hear the caller through the speaker.

Multitask

If you leave the call screen to use another program, a live call will be visible in the Status bar.

To return to the dial-up window:

- Drag down the Status bar and tap the call to open the Notification panel.

In order to end a call while multitasking:

- Drag down the Status bar and press End call to open the Notification panel.

Configurations for call pop-ups

When you receive a call while using another app, a pop-up message might be displayed.

- Click on More choices.
- After that, settings
- While using apps from the Phone menu, calls are displayed.

There are a number of options available:

• Full screen: Show an incoming call in the Phone app.

• Pop-up: If there is an incoming call, a pop-up will show up at the top of the screen.

• Mini pop-up: When an incoming call is made, a smaller pop-up will show.

• Keep calls in pop-up: Choose this option to keep calls that have been answered in a pop-up window.

Control calls

Telephone call history

Your phone chats are recorded in a log. You can block numbers, use voicemail, and set up speed dialing.

You can save a contact from a recent call

Utilize call information from recent calls to create or update your Contacts list.

1. From the Phone menu, choose Recents.

2. To save your Contacts list, click Add to Contacts on the call that contains the data you wish to save.

3. Choose a new or updated contact.

Remove call records

Follow these methods to remove anything from the Call log:

1. From the Phone menu, choose Recents.

2. Touch and hold the call you wish to remove from the Call log in order to choose it.

3. Choose Delete.

Block a digit

You won't receive any messages if you add a caller to your Block list because all subsequent calls from that number go directly to voicemail.

1. From the Phone menu, choose Recents.

2. Tap on the caller's number to choose who you wish to add.

3. From the Details menu, choose Block, and if prompted, click OK.

Altering your Block list is another option in Settings. From the Phone menu, select More, then Settings, and then Block numbers.

Swift dial

For quickly calling a default number, a contact can be given a shortcut number.

1. From the Phone menu, choose Keypad, More settings, then Speed dial. The Speed dial numbers screen shows the reserved speed dial numbers.

2. Decide on an unclaimed telephone number.

• Tap Menu to choose a different Speed dial number from the following one.

• The phone number's first digit is reserved for voicemail.

3. Enter a contact's name or choose Add from Contacts to add them to the number.

• The chosen contact is shown in the box for the Speed dial number.

To make a call, use Speed dial

Calls can be placed via speed dial.

• Keep pressing the phone's Speed dial number.

• Enter the first few digits of the speed dial number first, then hold down the last digit if it has more than one digit.

Delete a speed dial entry

A previously assigned Speed dial number can be removed.

1. From the Phone menu, choose More options, then Speed dial.

2. After choosing the contact, select Delete to remove it from your speed dial.

Calls Made in Case of Emergency

No matter if your phone is working or not, you can dial the local emergency number. If your phone is turned on, you can dial for help in an emergency.

1. After keying in the emergency phone number, click Call (911 in North America).

2. Conclude your call.

In this kind of call, you get access to the majority of in-call features. The emergency phone number can be called even if the phone is locked, allowing anyone to contact for assistance in an emergency.

The only available calling option while calling from a locked screen is emergency calling. The remaining components of the phone are secure.

Setting the phone

You can modify the settings for the Phone app using these choices.

- From the Phone menu, select More options, then Settings.

Call multiple parties at once

In the event that they are listed in your service plan, the following services are supported.

Make a call with several people

If your service plan permits it, you can place a call while one is already in progress.

1. From the active call, select Add call to place a second call.

2. After entering the new number, click the Call button.

Upon picking up the phone:

- Press Swap to alternate between the calls.
- To hear all of the callers at once, choose Merge (multi-conferencing).

Videos calls

Make a video call by doing the following:

- After inputting a phone number, select Phone, then Video or Duo call.

NOTE: Not all devices support video calling.

The recipient can choose to accept the video call or answer it as a conventional voice call.

Real Time Text (RTT)

Chat with the other person by typing back and forth over the phone in real time. You can utilize RTT while calling someone whose phone supports RTT or is linked to another teletypewriter (TTY) device.

The RTT indicator appears when an RTT call is incoming.

1. From the Phone menu, choose More options, followed by Settings.

2. From the drop-down menu, choose Real-time text to access the following choices:

• RTT call button: Control the visibility of the RTT call button.

• Make use of an external TTY keyboard. When connected, hide the RTT keyboard.

• TTY mode: Choose the ideal TTY setting for your existing keyboard.

New Samsung Note Notes

Use Samsung Notes to create text-based notes, audio recordings, songs, and images with footnotes.

You may easily share your notes via social networking services. In the Apps menu, select Add after selecting Samsung Notes.

Assign a title

Add an attachment

Set text options

Recordings of voice

Create voice recordings that can be used for meetings or lectures and include annotations.

While the audio is being captured, take notes. The playback and text scrolling are timed to each other.

1. Open Samsung Notes, then select Add.

2. From the menu for Insert, choose Voice recordings.

3. Write content using the text options while the audio is being recorded.

Note-taking options

It is possible to edit, organize, and manage notes. Samsung Notes offers the following substitutions:

• To import a PDF, open the file in Samsung Notes.

• Search: Use keywords to find information.

• More options

Edit: By choosing a note, you can share, delete, lock, save as a file, or transfer it.

Sort: Reverse the notes' chronological order.

View: Alternate between the List, Grid, and Simple List views.

To view what you've written, you can organize your notes into categories. To access the following choices in Samsung Notes, tap the Navigation drawer:

Access the settings for the Samsung Notes app. View the whole list of notes under "Notes."

• Regularly used: Easy access to frequently used notes.

• Shared notebooks: You can access shared notebooks with contacts using your Samsung account.

• Trash: Deleted notes are accessible in the trash for 15 days.

• Organize, add, and remove groups from folders.

Gmail Apps

It's possible that your smartphone already has the relevant Google apps loaded. You can download apps from the Google PlayTM store.

Chrome

Use ChromeTM to browse the internet and sync your open tabs, bookmarks, and address bar data from your computer to your mobile device.

Drive

You have access to your Google DriveTM cloud account's saved files and may open, view, rename, and share them.

Duo

One can make video calls.

Gmail

You can send and receive emails using Google's web-based email service.

Google

Utilize technology that recognizes your interests to find internet content. Activate your personalized feed to start receiving content that is relevant to you.

Maps

Obtain directions and other details regarding your current location. You have to do it.

Photos

Your pictures and videos are automatically stored and backed up by Google PhotosTM to your Google Account.

Play films and television shows

View the TV shows and movies you have purchased from Google Play. Videos that have been saved to your device can also be viewed.

Playing store

You can find brand-new games, apps, music, magazines, books, and TV shows in the Google Play store.

YouTube

You can use your device to directly watch and post YouTube videos. Browse and stream YouTube Music artists, albums, and playlists.

Microsoft programs

Microsoft may preload the following apps. Apps may be downloaded via the Galaxy shop and Play Store.

Outlook has a calendar, contacts, tasks, mail, and more.

LinkedIn

Find and connect with professionals from across the world.

Office

You can utilize the Excel, Word, and PowerPoint programs using the Microsoft Office mobile app.

OneDrive

In your free online OneDrive account, which you can access from any computer, tablet, or phone, you can save and share pictures, videos, documents, and other data.

Chapter Three: Wi-Fi Configuration

By connecting to a Wi-Fi network, you can access the Internet without using your mobile data.

1. From Settings, select Connections, then Wi-Fi. Press to activate Wi-Fi and search for networks.

2. Choose a network and type a password if necessary.

A private Wi-Fi network should be used to connect to

If a scan does not reveal your desired Wi-Fi network, you can still connect by manually entering the information.

Ask the WiFi network administrator for the password and name before you begin.

1. To activate Wi-Fi, press Connections in the Settings menu, followed by Wi-Fi.

2. Select Add network at the bottom of the list as you scroll.

3. Complete the following information about the wireless network:

• Network name: Specify the exact name of the network.

• Security: From the menu, select a security setting, and if required, enter a password.

• Auto reconnect: Choose this option if you want to rejoin to the network whenever you are within range.

• Advanced: List any additional choices, such as proxy settings and IP address.

Wi-Fi Advanced Settings

You can manage stored networks, connect to a range of Wi-Fi hotspots and networks, and check your device's network addresses.

1. Select Wi-Fi from the Connections menu in Settings and push to activate it.

2. Select Advanced, then More choices.

• Switch to mobile data: If this option is enabled, when the Wi-Fi connection is unstable, your device will use mobile data. In the event that the Wi-Fi signal gets strong, it switches back to Wi-Fi.

• Automatically activate Wi-Fi: Turn on Wi-Fi in locations that get a lot of traffic.

• Indicate the network's quality: Information on network stability and speed should be displayed.

• Network notification: Receive alerts when open networks are discovered nearby.

• Control networks

View saved Wi-Fi networks and decide whether to automatically connect to or ignore particular networks.

• Wi-Fi control history: View which applications have recently turned your Wi-Fi on or off.

• Hotspot 2.0: Automatically connect to WiFi networks that support Hotspot 2.0.

Install network certificates as well as authentication certificates.

• MAC address: Check your device's MAC address.

• IP address: Check your device's IP address.

Wireless Direct

Devices are able to exchange data using Wi-Fi Direct.

1. In Settings, choose Connections, then press Wi-Fi, and then tap to activate Wi-Fi.

2. From the menu, choose More options, then Wi-Fi Direct.

3. Choose a device and connect using the directions on the screen.

Cut off your Wi-Fi Direct connection.

Disconnect your device from any Wi-Fi

Direct devices it may be linked to. Click Connections, then select Wi-Fi.

There are more options after Wi-Fi Direct in the Settings menu. Tap a device to disconnect it.

Bluetooth

You can couple your device with other Bluetooth-capable gadgets like headsets or Bluetooth-enabled car systems.

Once a pairing is made, the devices can communicate without having to enter the passkey again since they remember each other.

1. Select Bluetooth from the Connections menu in Settings, then tap to activate Bluetooth.
2. After making your choice, connect your device by following the on-screen directions.

To use this feature when sharing a file, press Bluetooth.

Change a paired device's name

To make it simpler to recognize a paired device, it can be given a new name.

1. Select Bluetooth from the Connections menu in Settings, then tap to activate Bluetooth.

2. From the drop-down menu next to the device name, choose Settings, then Rename.

Unpair a Bluetooth device

The two devices lose the ability to recognize one another when you unpair them, and you must pair them once more in order to reconnect.

1. Select Bluetooth from the Connections menu in Settings, then tap to activate Bluetooth.

2. Hit Settings, then tap Unpair, next to the device.

Modern choices

More Bluetooth features are accessible through the Advanced menu.

1. From the Settings menu, choose Connections, then Bluetooth.

2. Click on More choices.

To have access to the following features, select Advanced:

Music sharing: Make your Bluetooth speaker or headphones available for use by others.

Ringtone synchronization: Use the ringtone you've chosen for your device when receiving calls over Bluetooth.

History of Bluetooth control

Examine the applications that have recently utilized Bluetooth.

You can communicate with other devices via Near Field Communication (NFC) without a network connection. Some payment apps, including Android Beam, employ this mechanism.

NFC compatibility and being four centimeters apart from the sending device are requirements for the receiving device.

To enable this option, go to Settings, hit Connections, followed by NFC and payment, and then press.

Google Beam

Use Android Beam to transfer contacts, pictures, or other files between NFC-capable smartphones.

1. Select Settings, then select Connections, NFC, and Payment. Press to enable NFV.

2. To use this feature, press Android Beam and then tap. Tap Android Beam to use this function while exchanging files.

Click and pay

Use a payment app that is NFC-compatible to complete transactions. Simply touch the device on a suitable card reader to accomplish this.

1. Select Settings, then select Connections, NFC and payment, and finally push to enable NFC.

2. To access the default payment app, select Payment, then tap Tap and Pay.

• Press, Tap, and pay with open apps to utilize another app in place of the default one if it is open.

• Tap Others, then select your favorite app to make another payment app the default.

Flying Mode

All network connections, including texting, Wi-Fi, calling, mobile data, and Bluetooth, are turned off when the device is in airplane mode.

Once enabled, you can use the Settings or Quick settings panel to turn on Bluetooth and Wi-Fi. To use this option, navigate to Settings, select Connections, and then tap Airplane mode.

Cellular networks

Set up your device's ability to use mobile data and connect to available mobile networks by using the mobile networks.

• Select Mobile networks under Connections under Settings.

• Data roaming: Choose whether you want your device to establish a connection to a mobile data network if you are outside of your network area.

• Network mode: Your mobile device's network modes are selectable.

• Access Point Names (APNs): These are the network configurations your device needs to connect to your provider; choose or add APNs.

• Network administrators: Select your favorite and available networks.

Utilize these capabilities to keep an eye on your connection's settings, which could have an impact on your bill.

Use of Data

Check your mobile data and Wi-Fi consumption.

Additionally, restrictions and cautions can be customized. Select Settings, then Connections, and finally Data use.

Switching on Data Saver

Use the Data Saver to reduce your data usage by preventing the specified apps from sending or receiving background data.

• Click Settings, then Connections, Data Usage, and finally Data Saver.

• To enable Data Saver, tap; to grant some apps free data usage while Data Saver is active, press Allow app.

To impose particular limits, press after each application.

Track mobile data

Set limitations and restrictions to control who can access your mobile data. Press Connections, then Data use, under Settings.

You'll see the following choices:

• Mobile data: Utilize the mobile data included in your plan.

• International data roaming: When traveling abroad, turn on your mobile data services.

• Mobile data usage: You can view the data usage statistics for a specific time frame for the mobile connection. Data use for apps is also visible.

• Billing cycle and data warning: Change the date in a month to correspond with your mobile carrier's billing date. Utilize these tools to keep an eye on your data usage.

Track the Wi-Fi information

When you modify the networks and use restrictions, you can limit your access to data.

1. Select Connections from the Settings menu, followed by Data use.

2. Select Wi-Fi data consumption to view the Wi-Fi networks' data usage patterns over time. You can also view the overall app usage.

Wireless Hotspot

The mobile hotspots create a Wi-Fi network that may be accessed by numerous devices using your network data plan.

1. Select Mobile Hotspot under Settings, followed by Connections, Mobile Hotspot, and Tethering.

2. Tap to turn on the mobile hotspot.

3. Turn on Wi-Fi on the linked device, then select your device's hotspot. Input the password to connect.

4. Click connected devices to get a list of connected devices.

Band

Select a band from the available selections.

1. Select Connections from the Settings menu, followed by Mobile Hotspot and Tethering.

2. Select any option by pressing Band. Set the mobile hotspot's settings.

The connection and security options for your mobile hotspot are customizable.

• Click connections, mobile hotspot, and tethering under settings, then click mobile hotspot.

• Select additional choices.

Then set up the portable hotspot for any of the subsequent:

• Name of the network: View and modify the name of your mobile hotspot.

• Hide my device: Prevent other gadgets from figuring out where your mobile hotspot is.

• Security: Choose the level of security for your mobile hotspot

• Password: You can view and modify your password if your security level uses one.

• Battery-saving mode: Examine the hotspot's traffic to determine how much power is being used.

• Safeguarded management frames

Turn on this function to receive additional privacy safeguards.

Timeout controls

The mobile hotspot can be set up to automatically turn off if no devices are connected.

1. Select connections, mobile hotspot, tethering, and then mobile hotspot under settings.

2. Select more choices

Choose an interval, then time out settings. Keep in mind that you may control how you use your data by using this function.

Internet sharing

Enable Wi-Fi sharing to rapidly share the network with another device.

1. From the Settings menu, choose Connections, followed by Mobile hotspot and tethering, and finally Mobile hotspot.

2. Select More options, then Wi-Fi sharing, to allow Wi-Fi sharing.

Mobile hotspot

Share your hotspot automatically with other devices that are signed into your Samsung account.

1. Select Mobile hotspot from the connections and tethering menu.

2. Select Auto hotspot and tap to turn on the feature.

Tethering

Tethering allows you to share your internet connection with other devices.

1. Select Settings, Connections, Mobile Hotspot, and Tethering.

2. Connect the device and the computer using a USB cable, then select USB tethering.

Device localization

You can rapidly connect with other nearby devices by turning on Nearby device scanning.

This feature will alert you if there are any connected devices that are available.

1. From the Settings menu, choose Connections, More connection settings, and Nearby device scanning.

2. Tap to make the feature active.

Connection to a printer

Connect your device to a printer that is part of a Wi-Fi network if you want to print photos and documents from it.

1. From the Settings menu, choose Connections, More connection settings, and Printing.

2. Choose Add printer under More options after choosing Default print service.

• If your printer requires a plugin, tap Download plugin and add a print service in accordance with the on-screen instructions. Keep in mind that not all apps are capable of printing.

You can connect your device to a secure private network via a virtual private network, or VPN.

You'll need the essential connection details from your VPN administrator.

1. From the Settings menu, choose Connections, More connection settings, and VPN.

2. Choose Add VPN profile, then choose More choices.

3. After entering the VPN's network information as given by the network administrator, tap Save.

A Virtual Private Network's administration

Go to the VPN's settings menu to delete or change the VPN.

1. From the Settings menu, choose Connections, More connection settings, and VPN.

2. Click Settings next to a VPN.

3. Edit the VPN and save your changes, or hit Delete to remove it.

Establishing a VPN connection

Once a VPN is set up, connecting to it and disconnecting from it is easy.

1. From the Settings menu, choose Connections, More connection settings, and VPN.

2. After choosing a VPN, connecting using your login information. Navigate to Settings, VPN, and then Disconnect to disconnect.

Personal DNS

Your device can be configured to utilize a private DNS server.

1. From the Settings menu, choose Connections, More connection settings, and Private DNS.

2. Select any offered choices to configure a private DNS.

3. Select the "Save" option.

Ethernet

You can still use an Ethernet cable to connect your device to a local network even if there isn't a wireless network connection available.

1. Use an Ethernet wire to connect your device to the internet.

2. Select Settings, followed by Connections, More connection settings, Ethernet, and then adhere to the on-screen prompts. An adaptor is required for Ethernet cable connection with your device.

Movements and Sounds

The noises and vibrations used to signal screen interactions and notifications are controllable.

In-ear mode

You may still alter your device's sound mode without using the volume keys.

• Select a mode by going to Settings > Sounds and Vibration:

•Sound: To receive alerts and notifications, use the vibrations, volume, and noises that you have selected in the Sound settings. You can configure your device to vibrate and ring simultaneously when you receive a call.

•Vibrate: Only utilize vibrations for notifications and alerts.

•Mute: Turn off your device's sound. Put a time restriction on the device's temporary mute setting.

Use the sound mode settings in place of the volume keys to change the sound model so that you don't lose your customized sound levels.

Simple silence

Simply flipping the gadget over or covering the screen can quickly muffle sounds.

Go to Settings and then click on Advanced features. Motions and gestures, followed by Simple mute and tapping to enable

Vibrations

Your device's vibration pattern and timing are both adjustable. To accomplish this, go to Settings, followed by Sounds and Vibration, and then Options.

The many choices consist of:

•Vibration pattern: Pick one of the vibration patterns that are already available.

•Vibration intensity: Use the sliders to adjust how loud notifications, calls, and interactions will vibrate.

Volume

- Set the volume for ringtones, notifications, and other sounds.
- Drag the sliders after selecting Settings, Sounds and Vibration, and Volume.
- Keep in mind that the Volume key can also be used to change the volume.
- Slide the volume controls to adjust every volume setting.

Use the volume controls for media

Change the default behavior of the Volume keys so that they control the media's overall volume instead of the sound type that is currently playing.

1. Select Volume under Settings, Sounds, and Vibration.

2. Tap Use Volume Keys for Media to make this feature active.

Media volume restrictions

When using Bluetooth speakers or headphones, keep the device's maximum volume output at a reasonable level.

1. Select Volume under Settings, Sounds, and Vibration.

2. From the drop-down menu, choose More options, then Media volume limit.

3. Tap to make this feature active.

To choose the maximum output volume, move the Custom volume limit slider. Touch Set volume limit PIN to make changing the volume subject to a PIN.

Ringtone

To customize your ringtone, just add your own or pick one from the pre-made options. Select Settings, followed by Sounds and Vibration, and then Ringtone.

Select your preferred ringtone by tapping any one and listening to its preview. To use an audio file as your ringtone instead, select Add.

Sound of Notification

Choose a sound theme for Samsung Keyboard, charging, and other touch-related interactions.

Select any desired option by going to Settings, Sounds and Vibration, then System sound.

Sound

When you tap the navigation buttons or touch and hold objects on the screen, the device vibrates. When you dial numbers on the phone keypad, the vibration feature activates. When you use gestures to navigate, the vibration feature activates.

• Samsung keyboard: The Samsung keyboard vibrates when you type.

Atmos Dolby

Enjoy the Dolby Atmos's quality when you are watching content that has been mixed especially for the system.

This feature might only be accessible if a headset is connected.

1. Select Sound and Vibration, then Sound quality and effects, from the Settings menu.

2. To experience the best audio, use Dolby Atmos.

Equalizer

Choose an audio preset that has been tailored for various musical genres. Alternately, you can manually adjust your audio's settings.

1. Select Sound quality and effect from the Sounds and vibration menu in Settings.

2. Tap Equalizer to choose a musical category.

Change Sound

Enhance the sound quality of your music for the best listening experience. Customize the sound for each ear to improve the audio experience.

1. Go to Settings then Sounds and vibration then Sound quality and effects then Adapt sound.

2. Go to the preferred sound profile, then tap Settings to personalize.

Control notifications

Notifications from apps and services can be customized.

• Tap Notifications from the Settings menu.

• Suggestions for actions and replies: Receive relevant suggestions for actions in response to notifications and replies.

• Swipe right or left to snooze: You can snooze a notification for a later time by swiping left or right.

• App icon badges: Use badges on app icons to identify which apps have current alerts.

• Toggle whether or not badges show the amount of unread notifications.

• Status bar: Change the number of notifications that appear in the Status bar.

• Do not disturb: When this mode is enabled, sounds and notifications are blocked. Configure exceptions for individuals, apps, and alerts.

Block the app notifications

Each app's notifications can be changed or disabled. Apps have different options.

1. Go to Settings then Notifications then See all.

2. Select an app to access the following options:

• Display notifications: Allow notifications from this app to be blocked.

• Categories: Set up notification options that are exclusive to this app.

• App icon badges: If there are alerts, display a badge on the icon.

Smart Alert

You can set the device to notify you about missed calls and messages by vibrating when you pick it up.

• From Settings, tap Advanced features then Motions and gestures then Smart alert, and tap to enable.

Smart pop-up view

Receive notifications as icons that can be tapped and expanded in pop-up view.

• From Settings, tap Advanced features then Smart pop-up view, and tap to enable.

Display

You can configure the screen font size, brightness, timeout delay, and many other display settings.

Dark mode

Dark mode allows you to choose to a darker theme to make your eyes more comfortable at night by dimming white or bright screens and notifications.

• Tap Display in Settings to get the following options:

• Light: Give your gadget a light color theme (default).

• Dark: Set your device to a dark color theme.

• Settings for Dark Mode: Control when and where Dark Mode is applied.

• Turn on as scheduled: Set Dark mode to Sunset to Sunrise or Custom schedule.

• Apply to wallpaper: When the wallpaper is active, the Dark mode settings are applied to it.

• Adaptive color filter: To reduce eye strain, turn on the Blue light filter automatically between sunset and sunrise.

Chapter Four: Gallery and Camera

You can take crisp pictures and film videos using the Camera app. Pictures and videos are saved in Gallery. You can see and change them right here.

Camera

Enjoy the professional-grade controls, video modes, and lenses.

- After selecting Apps, click Camera.

Double-press the Side key after launching Quick Launch to access the Camera app.

Settings — Zoom — Gallery — Capture — Shooting modes — Switch cameras

Examine the Camera display

Use your device's rear and front cameras to take stunning pictures.

1. Open Camera and configure it using the following choices:

- Press the desired screen to bring it into focus.
- When you do this, a brightness scale will be shown. Simply move this slider to alter brightness.
- To switch between the front and rear cameras, swipe either upwards or downwards.

- To switch to a different shooting mode, swipe either left or right.
- For other camera settings, go to Settings.

2. Click Capture.

Configure the shooting mode

Choose from a variety of shooting modes or let the camera decide the optimal mode.

- Swipe left or right after selecting Camera to go to another shooting mode.
- Single-take: Take numerous still images and video from diverse perspectives.
- Photo: Allow the camera to choose the ideal camera settings.
- Video: Let the camera decide what settings are best for videos.
- Additional: Choose from a number of shooting modes.
- Toggle between shooting modes, which are located in a tray at the bottom of the camera, by pressing Edit.

- Pro tip: Manually adjust the exposure value, ISO sensitivity, color tone, and white balance when taking pictures.
- Panorama: To create a linear image, take pictures either vertically or horizontally.
- Food: Snap pictures of it that show off its vivid colors.
- Night: Use this to take pictures in dim light without using the flash.
- Live focus: In your photos, alter the backdrop blurring to make the subject stand out.
- Live focus video: Modify the backdrop blur in the videos to highlight the subject.
- Professional video: While you are recording, manually adjust the exposure level, ISO sensitivity, color tone, and white balance of your videos. To observe slow motion in high-quality, record videos at a very high frame rate. Play a specific area of a video in slow motion after it has been captured.

- Slow motion: Take high frame rate videos if you want to see them in slow motion.
- Hyperlapse: To make a video time lapse, record at varying frame rates. Depending on the scene being recorded and the movement of the device, the frame rate is adjusted.

Actual Focus

By including interactive focus effects, you may make your images more engaging.

1. Select More after selecting Live focus from the Camera menu.

2. From the Live focus effect menu, choose an effect.

3. Drag the slider to adjust the settings.

4. Choose Capture.

Video capture

Utilize your device to capture high-definition videos.

1. In the Camera app, swipe left or right to access the Video shooting mode.

2. Press Record to begin recording a video.

3. Press Pause to take a brief break.

4. Click "Resume" to go further.

5. Press Stop when you're finished. Utilizing videos on your device

The Camera Presets

Utilize the icons on the settings menu and the primary camera to set up your camera.

The following can be accessed by selecting Settings from the Camera menu:

Intelligent capabilities

- Scene optimizer: Change the color parameters of your image to match the subject.
- Shot recommendations: These allow you to choose better shooting modes.
- Smart selfie angle: Automatically switch to a wide-angle lens when there are lots of people in the frame.

- Scan QR codes: The camera can automatically find QR codes.

Pictures

- Push the shutter button all the way out to: Every time you move the shutter to the closest edge, you can decide whether to make a GIF or a burst shot.
- Save choices: Choose the file formats that include additional saving choices.

HEIF images (Image)

Store the photographs as high efficiency pictures to make the most of your storage space.

Keeping RAW copies: Save duplicates of the images that were taken in Pro mode in RAW and JPEG.

Widespread form correction

With an extra wide lens, picture distortions are automatically corrected.

Videos

- Rear video size: For videos captured by the back camera, choose a video resolution and aspect ratio.
- Front video size: For videos taken with the front camera, choose a video resolution and aspect ratio.

Optimum video size

- Choose the resolution, aspect ratio, and frame rate for your video to give it a cinematic feel. Options for advanced recording: Improve the videos by using more modern recording formats.

High-performance video

- Use the HEVC format to record the videos in order to save space. Some devices or sharing websites might not be able to play back videos in this format.

In HDR10+ video

Record with HDR10+ to optimize your footage. This format must be supported by the playback devices.

- Video stabilization: Turn on Anti-shake to maintain the camera's focus while it is moving.

Featured functions

- Auto HDR: Take photos with additional detail in the dark or light sections of your scene.
- Selfie tone: Give your photos a cold or warm tint.
- Tracking auto-focus: Maintain sharp focus on a moving item.
- Photos as shown in previews: Save selfies as they appear in the previews.
- Grid lines: Use the viewfinder's grid lines to align a movie or a picture.
- Location tags: Give an image a GPS tag.

Procedures for shooting

The Volume key can be used to zoom, record videos, take images, and adjust the system volume. Press it to do any of these things.

- Use the voice recognition feature to capture pictures.
- Another shutter button should be placed so you can explore the screen.
- Reveal palm: Face the camera with your palm while taking photos.
- Settings to maintain: If you wish to start the camera with the same selfie angle, shooting mode, and filters that you used before, choose that option.
- Location for storage: Select a location for storage.
- To view the Storage location, a memory card must be installed.
- Sound shutter: Make a sound when taking a picture.
- Vibrations on touch: Press the Camera app screen to turn on vibrations.
- Change settings: Reset the camera's settings to their original state.

- Call us at: Use the Samsung Members to contact Samsung support.
- The camera: See the details about the apps and software.

Gallery

To view all the media saved on your device, go to Gallery. The movies and photographs can be viewed, edited, or managed.

- After selecting Apps, click Gallery.

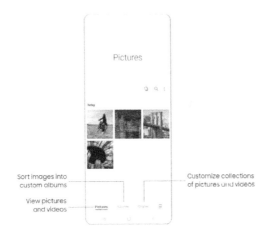

The Gallery app allows you to view the device photographs.

1. Select Pictures from the Gallery menu.

2. Click on an image to view it. To view further videos or pictures, swipe right or left.

Edit Pictures

Utilize the Gallery's editing features to make your photographs look better.

1. Select Pictures from the Gallery menu.

2. Click a photo to view it, then click Edit to get the following menu options:

- Transform the image by cropping, flipping, rotating, or making other adjustments.
- Add extra color effects with filters.
- Tone: Modify the brightness, contrast, exposure, and other settings.
- Overlay animated or illustrated stickers as a sticker.
- Draw: Include handwritten or hand-drawn information.
- Text: Add text to a picture.
- Auto adjust: Achieve better results with images by using automatic adjustments.

- Reset: Reverse the adjustments that have been made to return to the original image.

3. Press Save when you're finished.

Play Movie

Look at the recorded videos. The videos can be saved as favorites, and you can view more information about them.

1. Select Pictures from the Gallery menu.

2. Tap a video to watch it.

3. To view further videos and photographs, swipe to the right or left.

4. Press Play to begin a video.

Create Video

The videos you've saved on your smartphone can be edited.

1. Click Pictures under Gallery.

2. Press it to watch a video.

3. Use the Edit button to split the video into sections.

4. When done, click Save and then Confirm.

Share pictures and videos

Select Pictures from the Gallery app.

1. Choose Pictures from the Gallery option.

2. From the More options menu, choose Videos and Images, then click Share.

3. Click Share, then pick the connection or application you want to share your choice with. Obey the directions displayed on the screen.

Remove the videos and photos

Any pictures or movies on your smartphone should be deleted.

1. Click Edit under More choices in the Gallery menu.

2. Tap the images and videos to select them.

3. When asked, select Delete and then confirm.

Organize like-minded images

Sort the Gallery's movies and pictures in accordance with how similar they are.

1. Select Group Similar Images under Gallery.

2. Select Ungroup to return to the Gallery as it was the same Pictures.

Generate a screenshot

- Snap a picture of your screen.

Your phone will automatically create an album for Screenshots in the Gallery app. Press and then let go of the Side and Volume down buttons.

Configurations for a Screenshot

Adjust the settings for the screenshot.

- From the Settings menu, select Advanced features, followed by Screenshots and screen recorder.
- Toolbar for screenshots: Additional options are visible in this toolbar after taking a snapshot.

- Disable the status and navigation bars: Hide the status and navigation bars on screenshots.
- Delete shared screenshots: The screenshot toolbar allows you to automatically delete screenshots that have been shared.
- Format for screenshots: To save screenshots, select either PNG or JPG as the file type.

Made in the USA
Las Vegas, NV
06 August 2024

93448012R00075